101 *Farmhouse* FAVORITES

Fried Green Tomato Biscuits, page 15

Candy Apple Cheesecake, page 69

Sunflower Strawberry Salad, page 27

Gooseberry Patch
2545 Farmers Dr., #380
Columbus, OH 43235

www.gooseberrypatch.com
1·800·854·6673

Copyright 2012, Gooseberry Patch 978-1-62093-007-6
Second Printing, February, 2014

Gooseberry Patch *cookbooks*

Chicken & Wild Rice Soup, page 22

Chocolate Scotcheroos, page 90

Since 1992, we've been publishing our own country cookbooks for every kitchen and for every meal of the day! Each title has hundreds of budget-friendly recipes, using ingredients you already have on hand in your pantry.

In addition, you'll find helpful tips and ideas on every page, along with our hand-drawn artwork and plenty of personality. Their lay-flat binding makes them so easy to use...they're sure to become a fast favorite in your kitchen.

Call us toll-free at
1•800•854•6673
and we'd be delighted to tell you all about our newest titles!

Shop with us online anytime at
www.gooseberrypatch.com

Send us your favorite recipe!

and the memory that makes it special for you!* If we select your recipe for a brand-new **Gooseberry Patch** cookbook, your name will appear right along with it...and you'll receive a FREE copy of the book!

Submit your recipe on our website at
www.gooseberrypatch.com

Or mail to:

Gooseberry Patch • Attn: Cookbook Dept.
2545 Farmers Dr., #380 • Columbus, OH 43235

*Please include the number of servings and all other necessary information!

Have a taste for more?

Visit **www.gooseberrypatch.com**
to join our **Circle of Friends**!

- Free recipes, tips and ideas plus a complete cookbook index
- Get special email offers and our monthly eLetter delivered to your inbox
- Find local stores with **Gooseberry Patch** cookbooks, calendars and organizers

Pulled Pork Barbecue, page 62

Quick & Easy Lemon Bars, page 68

Crescent Breakfast Casserole, page 8

Tomato-Garbanzo Salad, page 21

Maple Pork Chops, page 51

Roasted Tomato-Feta Broccoli, page 45

Super Berry Crisp, page 75

CONTENTS

Old-Time Corncob Jelly, page 93

Dedication

To all our friends who love savoring every bite of a delicious, home-cooked meal and treasure old-fashioned recipes passed down for generations.

Appreciation

Endless thanks to all the wonderful cooks that sent in their tastiest recipes… we loved building this farmhouse collection!

Black Forest Brownie Sundae, page 73

Blueberry French Toast

2 c. fresh or frozen blueberries
2 T. cornstarch
1/4 c. sugar
1/2 c. orange juice
1/2 c. plus 3 T. water, divided
3 eggs
6 slices bread
2 T. butter, melted
cinnamon-sugar to taste

Place blueberries in a greased 13"x9" baking pan. In a bowl, combine cornstarch, sugar, orange juice and 1/2 cup water; pour over blueberries. Beat together eggs and remaining water in a shallow dish. Dip bread slices in egg mixture; place on top of blueberries in pan. Brush bread slices with butter and sprinkle with cinnamon-sugar. Bake at 350 degrees for 15 to 20 minutes, until bread is lightly toasted and blueberries are bubbly and thickened. Serve toast topped with blueberries. Serves 6.

7

Gloria Kaufmann
Orrville, OH

A new and yummy twist on a breakfast casserole that my whole family enjoys.

Crescent Breakfast Casserole

8-oz. tube refrigerated crescent
    rolls
6 to 8 eggs, beaten
1/4 c. milk
3/4 c. finely shredded Cheddar
    cheese
1/2 c. bacon or ground pork
    sausage, cooked and crumbled
salt and pepper to taste

Line the bottom and sides of a lightly
greased 13"x9" baking pan with
unrolled crescents, pinching seams
together to seal. In a bowl, mix
together remaining ingredients. Pour
over dough in baking pan. Bake at
350 degrees for about 20 minutes,
until golden and center is set.
Serves 8.

Tammy Walker
Kansas City, MO

This is a quick & easy
breakfast casserole for a
chilly morning or a hearty,
filling supper.

Country Sausage & Apples

1-lb. pkg. smoked pork sausage,
  sliced into 1-inch pieces
3 Granny Smith apples, cored
  and diced
1 c. brown sugar, packed
1/4 to 1/2 c. water

Place sausage in a slow cooker; top
with apples. Sprinkle with brown
sugar and drizzle water over all.
Stir gently; cover and cook on high
setting for 1-1/2 to 2 hours, until
apples are tender. Makes 4 servings.

9

Donna Maltman
Toledo, OH

A truly delicious
slow-cooker recipe. There's
just something about the
combination of sausage and
apples that tastes so good!

Apple Fritter Pancakes

1 c. all-purpose flour
1/4 t. salt
2 t. baking powder
1 egg, beaten
1 c. milk
1 T. oil
1/2 c. applesauce
1/2 t. nutmeg
1 t. cinnamon-sugar
Garnish: butter, powdered sugar

Combine all ingredients except garnish in a bowl; mix well. Drop batter by 1/4 cupfuls onto a greased griddle set over medium heat. Flip pancakes when tops start to bubble. Continue to cook until both sides are golden. Serve topped with butter and powdered sugar. Makes 6 servings.

Becky Raver
Goshen, KY

I accidentally made this recipe when I was low on oil and substituted applesauce...they turned out delicious!

Country Cabin Pancake Syrup

Rita Morgan
Pueblo, CO

Slip a jar of this
delectable syrup into a
basket along with some
pancake mix...a welcome
surprise for neighbors.

2 16-oz. pkgs. dark
   brown sugar
1 c. sugar
1/2 t. salt
4 c. water
3/4 c. corn syrup
1 T. maple extract

Combine all ingredients except
extract in a saucepan. Bring to
a boil over medium heat; boil
for about 10 minutes, stirring
constantly, until sugars are dissolved
and mixture is thickened. Let cool
to lukewarm; stir in extract. Place
in a covered container; keep
refrigerated for up to 4 weeks. Makes
about 7 cups.

11

Country Ham Biscuits

2 c. self-rising flour
1/2 c. plus 3 T. butter, divided
1 c. cooked ham, ground
1-1/2 c. shredded sharp Cheddar
   cheese
3/4 c. plus 2 T. buttermilk

Add flour to a bowl. Cut in 1/2 cup
butter with a pastry cutter or fork
until mixture resembles coarse
crumbs. Stir in ham and cheese.
Add buttermilk; stir with fork until
a moist dough forms. Drop dough by
heaping teaspoonfuls onto a lightly
greased baking sheet. Bake at
450 degrees for 10 to 13 minutes,
until lightly golden. Melt remaining
butter and brush over hot biscuits.
Makes 2 to 3 dozen.

Terri Scungio
Williamsburg, VA

I usually make these
biscuits with sausage,
but recently I tried
country ham instead...
everyone loved them!

Easy Bacon Frittata

3 T. oil
2 c. frozen shredded hashbrowns
7 eggs, beaten
2 T. milk
12 slices bacon, crisply cooked
  and crumbled
3/4 c. shredded Cheddar cheese

Heat oil in a large skillet over medium heat. Add hashbrowns and cook for 10 to 15 minutes, stirring often, until golden. In a bowl, whisk together eggs and milk. Pour egg mixture over hashbrowns in skillet; sprinkle with bacon. Cover and reduce heat to low. Cook for 10 minutes, or until eggs are set. Sprinkle with cheese; remove from heat, cover, and let stand about 5 minutes, until cheese is melted. Cut into wedges to serve. Makes 6 servings.

13

Beth Bundy
Long Prairie, MN
Delicious and oh-so simple to put together! Pair with fruit salad for brunch or a crisp green salad for an easy dinner.

Spinach Quiche

12-oz. pkg. frozen spinach
  soufflé, thawed
2 eggs, beaten
3 T. milk
2 t. onion, chopped
3/4 c. Italian ground pork
  sausage, browned and drained
1/2 c. sliced mushrooms
3/4 c. shredded Swiss cheese
9-inch pie crust, baked

In a bowl, mix together all
ingredients except crust; pour into
crust. Bake at 400 degrees for 30 to
45 minutes, until golden and center
is set. Cut into wedges. Serves 6.

Glenda Tolbert
Moore, SC
This is my go-to recipe for
brunches and get-togethers.
No matter where I bring it,
everyone always asks me
for the recipe!

Fried Green Tomato Biscuits

16-oz. tube refrigerated
   buttermilk biscuits
1/2 lb. bacon
1 c. buttermilk
1-1/2 c. self-rising cornmeal
salt and pepper to taste
2 green tomatoes, thickly sliced
Garnish: mayonnaise

Bake biscuits according to package
directions; set aside. In a large skillet,
cook bacon until crisp; remove to
paper towels to drain, reserving
drippings in skillet. Pour buttermilk
into a shallow bowl. On a small plate,
combine cornmeal, salt and pepper.
Dip tomato slices into buttermilk
and then cornmeal mixture, until
thickly coated on both sides. Fry
tomatoes in reserved drippings over
medium-high heat for 4 minutes
per side, or until golden. Drain on
paper towels. Split biscuits; spread
one biscuit half with mayonnaise.
Top with a tomato slice, bacon and
top half of biscuit. Serves 4 to 8.

15

Carol Hickman
Kingsport, TN

These southern classics
are great for a summertime
breakfast or brunch! Try
one with a tall glass
of sweet tea.

Swirled Coffee Cake

18-1/4 oz. pkg. yellow cake mix
5-1/4 oz. pkg. instant pistachio
    pudding mix
4 eggs, beaten
1 t. vanilla extract
1 c. water
1/2 c. oil
1/2 c. sugar
2 t. cinnamon
1/2 c. chopped walnuts

Combine dry cake mix and dry pudding mix in a large bowl; blend in eggs, vanilla, water and oil. Pour half the batter into a greased Bundt® pan; set aside. Mix together sugar, cinnamon and walnuts in a small bowl; sprinkle half over batter in pan. Swirl in with a knife; add remaining batter. Swirl in remaining sugar mixture. Bake at 350 degrees for 50 minutes, or until cake tests done with a toothpick. Cool in pan and remove to a serving platter. Makes 12 to 15 servings.

Carol Doiron
North Berwick, ME

A boxed mix makes this delicious coffee cake a breeze to prepare!

Baked Shrimp & Grits

5 c. water
1-1/4 c. quick-cooking grits,
  uncooked
2 c. shredded Cheddar cheese
1/2 c. butter
2 eggs, beaten
1 c. milk
garlic powder and salt to taste
1 lb. uncooked medium shrimp,
  peeled and cleaned
2 T. olive oil
1/2 c. white wine or chicken
  broth
2 t. garlic, minced
1-1/2 t. fresh parsley, chopped
1/4 t. salt
1/2 t. pepper
4 T. lemon juice

17

Bring water to a boil in a saucepan
over medium-high heat. Cook grits
in boiling water for 5 minutes. Add
cheese, butter, eggs, milk, garlic
powder and salt to grits; mix well.
Spoon into a greased 4-quart
casserole dish. Bake, uncovered, at
350 degrees for 45 minutes, or until
lightly golden. Meanwhile, in a skillet
over medium heat, sauté shrimp in
olive oil until cooked through. Add
remaining ingredients; heat through.
Top grits with shrimp before serving.
Serves 4 to 6.

Judy Zechman
Butler, PA

This recipe is a
grits-lover's dream come
true! It's so savory and
tasty, but still really
easy to prepare.

Impossibly Easy BLT Pie

12 slices bacon, crisply cooked
   and crumbled
1 c. shredded Swiss cheese
1/2 c. biscuit baking mix
1/3 c. plus 2 T. mayonnaise,
   divided
3/4 c. milk
1/8 t. pepper
2 eggs, beaten
1 c. shredded lettuce
6 thin slices tomato

Layer bacon and cheese in a lightly
greased 9-inch pie plate. In a bowl,
whisk together baking mix, 1/3 cup
mayonnaise, milk, pepper and eggs
until blended. Pour over cheese.
Bake at 350 degrees for 25 to
30 minutes, until top is golden and
a knife inserted in center comes out
clean. Let stand 5 minutes. Spread
remaining mayonnaise over pie.
Sprinkle with lettuce; arrange tomato
slices over lettuce. Serves 6.

Athena Colegrove
Big Springs, TX
I delighted my family
one morning with this
super-simple breakfast.
We all like BLT's, so we
really love this pie!

Sweet Apple Butter Muffins

1-3/4 c. all-purpose flour
1/3 c. plus 2 T. sugar, divided
2 t. baking powder
1/2 t. cinnamon
1/4 t. nutmeg
1/4 t. salt
1 egg, beaten
3/4 c. milk
1/4 c. oil
1 t. vanilla extract
1/3 c. apple butter
1/3 c. chopped pecans

Combine flour, 1/3 cup sugar, baking powder, spices and salt in a large bowl; set aside. In a separate bowl, blend egg, milk, oil and vanilla together; stir into flour mixture. Spoon one tablespoon batter into each of 12 paper-lined muffin cups; top with one teaspoon apple butter. Fill muffin cups 2/3 full using remaining batter; set aside. Toss pecans with remaining sugar; sprinkle evenly over muffins. Bake at 400 degrees until a toothpick inserted in the center tests clean, about 20 minutes. Makes one dozen.

The Inn At Shadow Lawn
Middletown, RI

The center of each muffin is filled with a spoonful of apple butter...yummy!

19

Brandi's Ultimate Tex-Mex Soup

1 T. olive oil
1 c. onion, diced
1 carrot, peeled and finely grated
1 T. ancho chili powder
1 T. garlic, minced
1-1/2 t. ground cumin
1 t. dried oregano
salt and pepper to taste
4 c. vegetable broth
13-oz. can chicken, drained
1 c. frozen corn, thawed
15-oz. can fire-roasted diced
    tomatoes
28-oz. can black beans, drained
    and rinsed
15-oz. can garbanzo beans,
    drained and rinsed
Garnish: sour cream, chopped
    fresh cilantro, lime wedges

Heat oil in a large stockpot over medium-high heat. Sauté onion in oil until golden and tender, 5 to 8 minutes. Add carrot and seasonings; cook one to 2 minutes. Add broth, chicken, corn, tomatoes with juice and beans. Cook over low heat for 25 to 30 minutes. Garnish as desired. Serves 6 to 8.

Brandi Howell
Owego, NY

During the winter months, my husband and I like to retreat to the couch and enjoy a bowl of this comforting soup while watching movies.

Tomato-Garbanzo Salad

1 c. elbow macaroni, uncooked
15-oz. can garbanzo beans,
   drained and rinsed
2 c. tomatoes, diced
1 c. celery, diced
1/2 c. red onion, diced
1/3 c. olive oil
1/4 c. lemon juice
2 T. fresh parsley, chopped
2 t. ground cumin
2 t. salt
1/2 t. pepper

Cook macaroni according to
package directions; drain and rinse
in cold water. Transfer to a large
bowl and combine with remaining
ingredients. Stir to mix well. Cover
and chill at least one hour. Makes
6 servings.

21

**Aubrey Dufour
Salem, IN**

Try this tasty salad the
next time you're looking
for something new to tote
to a get-together.

Chicken & Wild Rice Soup

6 c. water
6-oz. pkg. long grain and wild
   rice mix
2-oz. pkg. chicken noodle
   soup mix
2 stalks celery, sliced
1 carrot, peeled and chopped
1/2 c. onion, chopped
2 10-3/4 oz. cans cream of
   chicken soup
2 c. cooked chicken, chopped
salt and pepper to taste

Bring water to a boil in a large
stockpot over medium-high heat.
Stir in rice mix with seasoning
packet and noodle soup mix. Bring
to a boil. Cover and simmer over
medium-low heat for 10 minutes,
stirring occasionally. Add celery,
carrot and onion. Cover and simmer
10 minutes, stirring occasionally. Mix
in soup, chicken, salt and pepper.
Cover and simmer 10 minutes more,
stirring occasionally, until rice and
vegetables are tender. Serves 6.

Olivia Gust
Woodburn, OR

This soup is great on
a cold winter's day,
served with homemade bread
right out of the oven.

Summer in a Bowl

4 roma tomatoes, seeded
  and chopped
1 cubanelle pepper, seeded
  and chopped
1 cucumber, chopped
1/4 c. red onion, minced
6 fresh basil leaves, shredded
salt and pepper to taste
4 c. Italian bread, sliced, cubed
  and toasted
3 T. olive oil

Combine vegetables, basil, salt
and pepper in a bowl. Let stand at
room temperature for 30 minutes.
At serving time, stir in bread cubes;
drizzle with oil. Mix thoroughly;
serve at room temperature.
Serves 4.

23

Angie Cornelius
Sheridan, IL

We have a large, wonderful
vegetable garden every
summer. This salad makes
excellent use of all
those peppers, cucumbers
and tomatoes.

Best-Ever Spinach Salad

1 bunch fresh spinach, torn
6 eggs, hard-boiled, peeled
   and sliced
1 lb. bacon, crisply cooked
   and crumbled
1/2 c. olive oil
1/4 c. sugar
2 T. cider vinegar
1/2 t. salt
1/4 t. dry mustard
Optional: 1 T. dried, minced
   onion

In a large bowl, combine spinach,
eggs and bacon. In a separate bowl,
whisk together remaining ingredients.
Before serving, drizzle dressing over
spinach mixture and toss lightly to
coat. Serves 8 to 10.

Pamela Forrester
Pontoon Beach, IL
Everyone loves this salad,
even kids and people who say
they don't like spinach!

Mommy's Pasta Fagioli

3/4 c. onion, diced
3/4 c. celery, diced
2 T. butter
8 c. chicken broth
28-oz. can tomato purée
1/2 t. dried thyme
1 t. dried rosemary
salt and pepper to taste
2 15-oz. cans cannellini beans,
   drained and rinsed
2 c. ditalini pasta, cooked

In a stockpot over medium heat,
sauté onion and celery in butter
until onion is translucent. Add
broth, tomato purée and seasonings.
Simmer over low heat for one hour.
Add beans and pasta to soup; heat
through. Ladle into bowls to serve.
Serves 8.

25

Danielle Jowdy
South Salem, NY

This is a classic family
recipe that was passed
from my grandma, to my mom,
then to me. It is very light,
very flavorful and full
of memories.

Zesty Minestrone

1 lb. Italian pork sausage
   links, sliced
2 t. oil
1 onion, chopped
1 green pepper, chopped
3 cloves garlic, chopped
28-oz. can whole tomatoes
2 potatoes, diced
1/4 c. fresh parsley, chopped
2 t. dried oregano
1 t. dried basil
1 t. fennel seed
1/2 t. red pepper flakes
salt and pepper to taste
4 c. beef broth
2 16-oz. cans kidney beans
1 c. elbow macaroni, uncooked

Sauté sausage in oil in a large saucepan over medium heat; drain. Add onion, green pepper and garlic; cook 5 minutes. Add tomatoes with juice, potatoes, seasonings and broth; bring to a boil. Reduce heat; simmer 30 minutes. Stir in undrained beans and macaroni; simmer an additional 10 minutes, or until macaroni is tender. Makes 6 to 8 servings.

Beth Hagopian
Huntsville, AL

This hearty soup reheats well and is the perfect addition to any lunchbox.

Sunflower Strawberry Salad

2 c. strawberries, hulled and
   sliced
1 apple, cored and diced
1 c. seedless green grapes,
   halved
1/2 c. celery, thinly sliced
1/4 c. raisins
1/2 c. strawberry yogurt
2 T. sunflower kernels
Optional: lettuce leaves

In a large bowl, combine fruit,
celery and raisins. Stir in yogurt.
Cover and chill one hour. Sprinkle
with sunflower kernels just before
serving. Spoon over lettuce leaves,
if desired. Makes 6 servings.

27

Sister Toni Spencer
Watertown, SD

A great chilled
salad...super for hot
summer days!

Hearty Vegetable Soup

2 T. olive oil
1 onion, chopped
2 cloves garlic, minced
2 to 3 parsnips, peeled and
  thinly sliced
3 to 4 stalks celery, thinly sliced
3 carrots, peeled and thinly
  sliced
1 t. dried thyme
1/2 c. wild rice, uncooked
1/2 c. pearled barley, uncooked
7 to 8 c. beef broth
2 c. water
3 potatoes, peeled and cubed
1 tomato, diced
1 bunch fresh spinach, trimmed
salt and pepper to taste

Heat oil in a Dutch oven over
medium heat. Add onion, garlic,
parsnips, celery, carrots and thyme.
Cook, stirring frequently, until
vegetables softened. Stir in rice,
barley, broth, water, potatoes and
tomato. Cover and bring to a boil.
Reduce heat to medium-low.
Simmer, stirring occasionally, for
one hour. Stir in remaining
ingredients. Simmer for 2 to
3 minutes longer. Serves 6 to 8.

Cheryl Hambleton
Delaware, OH

Served with thick crusty
bread, this soup makes a
hearty and delicious meal.

Cabbage-Tomato Slaw

1 head cabbage, chopped
1 sweet onion, chopped
2 tomatoes, diced
1/2 c. mayonnaise
salt and pepper to taste

Combine all ingredients in a large
salad bowl. Toss to mix; cover and
refrigerate until serving time. Toss
again before serving. Makes 6 to
8 servings.

29

Tamara Parlor
Hazelhurst, GA

This simple slaw
tastes even better
the next day!

Pea Salad

1 c. elbow macaroni, cooked
3 slices bacon, crisply cooked
  and crumbled
1/2 c. green onion, chopped
2 c. frozen baby peas, thawed
1 c. mayonnaise
1/2 c. shredded Cheddar cheese

In a bowl, combine macaroni,
bacon, green onions and peas. Stir
in mayonnaise; cover and refrigerate
for at least 2 hours. Sprinkle with
cheese just before serving.
Serves 4 to 6.

Dee Faulding
Santa Barbara, CA

This is a great salad
to bring to any summer
gathering or a sunny
picnic in the park!

The Best Chicken Noodle Soup

16-oz. pkg. thin egg noodles,
    uncooked
12 c. chicken broth
1-1/2 T. salt
1 t. poultry seasoning
1 c. celery, chopped
1 c. onion, chopped
1 c. carrot, peeled and chopped
1/3 c. cornstarch
1/4 c. cold water
4 c. cooked chicken, diced

Cook noodles according to package directions; drain and set aside. Meanwhile, combine broth, salt and poultry seasoning in a very large pot; bring to a boil over medium heat. Stir in vegetables; reduce heat, cover and simmer for 15 minutes, or until vegetables are tender. Combine cornstarch with cold water in a small bowl; gradually add to soup, stirring constantly until thickened. Stir in chicken and noodles; heat through, about 5 to 10 minutes. Serves 8 to 10.

31

Evelyn Belcher
Monroeton, PA

My daughter gave me
this recipe years ago...
now it's my favorite!

Fresh Ranch Dressing

2 c. mayonnaise
1/2 c. milk
1-1/2 t. vinegar
1/4 t. Worcestershire sauce
1 green onion, finely chopped
1/3 c. grated Parmesan cheese
1/4 t. dill weed
1/8 t. pepper

Whisk together all ingredients in a large bowl. Pour into a large jar with a tight-fitting lid. Secure lid and store in refrigerator up to 2 weeks. Makes 4 cups.

Barbara Voight
Pound, WI

Making your own fresh salad dressing is easy! We enjoy this spooned over baked potatoes too.

Apple-Walnut Chicken Salad

6 c. mixed field greens or
    baby greens
2 c. deli roast chicken,
    shredded
1/3 c. crumbled blue cheese
1/4 c. chopped walnuts, toasted
1 Fuji or Gala apple, cored and
    chopped

In a large salad bowl, toss together all ingredients. Drizzle Balsamic Apple Vinaigrette over salad, tossing gently to coat. Serve immediately. Makes 6 servings.

Balsamic Apple Vinaigrette:

2 T. frozen apple juice
    concentrate
1 T. cider vinegar
1 T. white balsamic vinegar
1 t. Dijon mustard
1/4 t. garlic powder
1/3 c. olive oil

Whisk together all ingredients in a small bowl.

Becky Butler
Keller, TX

This tasty recipe uses the convenience of a roast chicken from your grocery store's deli...what a great time-saver!

Wash-Day Stew

1-1/2 lbs. stew beef, cubed
1/2 c. frozen mixed vegetables,
   thawed
1 c. water
28-oz. can stewed tomatoes
1 T. salt
2 T. sugar
1/2 c. celery, sliced
1/2 c. onion, chopped
2 c. potatoes, peeled and diced
1 c. carrot, peeled and diced

Place all ingredients into a 6-quart
Dutch oven. Cover and bake at
350 degrees for 4 hours. Stir stew;
cover and bake for an additional
3 hours. May also be prepared in a
slow cooker on low setting for
8 hours. Serves 6 to 8.

Sandra Crook
Jacksonville, FL

When I was young, we had no
washing machine...washing
clothes took all day! When
all the work was done, this
stew would be ready for all
the hungry wash women.

Minty Melon Salad

1 c. water
3/4 c. sugar
3 T. lime juice
1-1/2 t. fresh mint, chopped
5 c. watermelon, cubed
3 c. cantaloupe, cubed
3 c. honeydew, cubed
2 c. nectarines, pitted and sliced
1 c. blueberries
Garnish: fresh mint sprigs

Combine water, sugar, juice and mint in a saucepan; bring to a boil. Boil for 2 minutes, stirring constantly. Remove from heat; cover and cool completely. Combine fruit in a large bowl. Pour cooled dressing over fruit; stir until well coated. Cover and chill for at least 2 hours, stirring occasionally. Drain liquid before serving. Garnish with fresh mint sprigs. Serves 8 to 10.

35

Vickie

The spicy, fresh mint really brings out the sweetness of the juicy melon in this bright & cheery salad.

Baked Potato Soup

6 slices bacon, diced
3 c. potatoes, peeled and cubed
14-1/2 oz. can chicken broth
1 carrot, peeled and grated
1/2 onion, chopped
1 T. dried parsley
1/2 t. celery seed
1/2 t. salt
1/2 t. pepper
3 T. all-purpose flour
3 c. milk
1/4 lb. pasteurized process cheese
   spread, cubed
Garnish: thinly sliced green
   onions, additional crumbled
   bacon

In a large saucepan, cook bacon until crisp; drain. Add potatoes, broth, carrot, onion and seasonings. Cover and simmer until potatoes are tender, about 15 minutes. In a bowl, whisk together flour and milk until smooth; add to soup. Bring to a boil. Cook and stir for 2 minutes. Add cheese; stir until cheese melts. Ladle into bowls; garnish with green onions and bacon. Serves 8.

Diane Hixon
Niceville, FL

My daughter and I made this soup many times a day for our small cafe. It was our biggest seller...I can still see my daughter peeling all those potatoes!

Fresh Kale Salad

3 T. honey
1/2 c. olive or canola oil
juice of 1 lemon
pepper to taste
1 bunch fresh kale, torn and
   stems removed
1/2 c. raisins or dried cranberries
1/4 c. sunflower kernels

In a large bowl, combine honey,
oil, lemon juice and pepper. Whisk
until blended. Add kale and toss to
coat; let stand about 5 minutes.
Sprinkle with raisins or cranberries
and sunflower seeds; toss again.
Serves 6.

37

Carol Werner
Brooklyn Park, MN
This recipe goes together
so quickly, is very healthy
and tasty to boot!

Cool Summer Salad

1 cucumber, sliced
2 to 3 tomatoes, diced
1/4 red onion, thinly sliced
1 avocado, halved, pitted
  and cubed
1/2 c. Italian salad dressing

Combine all vegetables in a bowl.
Drizzle salad dressing over top.
Refrigerate, covered, for at least
one hour. Toss gently before serving.
Serves 4 to 6.

Chris Lercel
Covina, CA

This is a quick and tasty
salad we pull together
from our backyard garden.
It's great for potlucks
and picnics because it
travels well.

Spicy Black-Eyed Pea Soup

4 slices bacon, diced
1 green pepper, chopped
1 onion, chopped
2 cloves garlic, minced
2 15-1/2 oz. cans black-eyed peas
2 14-1/2 oz. cans diced tomatoes
1 c. water
1-1/4 t. ground cumin
1-1/4 t. dry mustard
1 t. chili powder
1/2 t. curry powder
1/2 t. pepper
1/4 t. sugar
Garnish: shredded Monterey
    Jack cheese

In a large saucepan over medium
heat, cook bacon until crisp. Remove
bacon to paper towels to drain,
reserving one tablespoon drippings
in saucepan. In drippings, sauté
green pepper, onion and garlic until
tender. Add peas with liquid,
tomatoes with juice, water and
seasonings. Bring to a boil. Reduce
heat, cover and simmer for 15 to
20 minutes. Garnish individual
servings with reserved bacon and
cheese. Serves 6 to 8.

Sheila Murray
Tehachapi, CA
This tastes so good! I like
to serve it with cornbread
that's topped with a big
dollop of honey-butter.

Luke's Tortellini Salad

16-oz. pkg. refrigerated cheese
  tortellini, uncooked
2 green peppers, chopped
2 c. cherry tomatoes, halved
6-oz. can sliced black olives,
  drained
16-oz. bottle light Italian salad
  dressing
1 c. grated Parmesan cheese

Cook tortellini according to package
directions; drain and rinse with cold
water. Transfer to a large bowl; let
cool in refrigerator. Once tortellini
is cooled, mix in peppers, tomatoes
and olives. Stir in salad dressing to
taste and cheese just before serving.
Serves 4.

Meg Dickinson
Champaign, IL
My friend Luke brought this
salad to a cookout, and I've
been making it ever since.
It's easy, delicious and
full of color too.

Cheesy Chicken Chowder

32-oz. can chicken broth
2 c. potatoes, peeled and diced
1 c. carrot, peeled and thinly
   sliced
1/2 c. onion, diced
1 t. salt
1/4 t. pepper
1/4 c. butter
1/3 c. all-purpose flour
2 c. milk
2 c. shredded sharp Cheddar
   cheese
2 c. cooked chicken, chopped
15-oz. can corn, drained

41

Bring broth to a simmer in a large
stockpot over medium heat. Add
vegetables, salt and pepper; cook
until tender. Melt butter in a separate
saucepan; add flour and whisk until
smooth. Gradually add milk to butter
mixture; cook and stir until mixture
starts to thicken. Add to stockpot;
stir until well mixed. Add cheese; stir
until melted. Add chicken and corn.
Simmer until heated through, about
3 to 5 minutes. Serves 6.

Ann Cass
Danielsville, GA
This recipe is to honor
my Aunt Mildred who lovingly
made it for me when I was
sick...it really does make
you feel better!

Ham & Bean Soup

1 c. dried navy beans
8 c. water, divided
2 stalks celery, sliced
2 carrots, peeled and sliced
1 onion, chopped
3/4 c. cooked ham, cubed
1 t. chicken bouillon granules
1 t. dried thyme
2 bay leaves
1/4 t. pepper

In a large saucepan, combine beans and 4 cups water. Bring to a boil; reduce heat to low. Simmer, uncovered, for 2 minutes. Remove from heat. Cover and let stand for one hour. Drain and rinse beans; return to pan. Add remaining water and remaining ingredients. Bring to a boil; reduce heat to low. Cover and simmer for 1-1/4 hours, or until beans are tender. Discard bay leaves. Using a fork, slightly mash some beans against the side of the saucepan to thicken soup. Makes 4 servings.

Kathy Grashoff
Fort Wayne, IN

Our family really enjoys this soup. It's always a welcome lunch after a chilly day in the stands watching football!

Dan's Broccoli & Cheese Soup

16-oz. pkg. frozen chopped
   broccoli, thawed
10-3/4 oz. cream of mushroom
   soup
1 c. milk
1 c. half-and-half
8-oz. pkg. cream cheese, cubed
1-1/2 c. pasteurized process
   cheese spread, cubed
garlic powder and pepper to taste

Combine all ingredients in a slow
cooker. Cover and cook on high
setting for 30 to 40 minutes. Reduce
to low setting; cover and cook for
an additional 3 to 4 hours, stirring
occasionally. Serves 6.

43

Dan Ferren
Sheridan, IN

By boss used to make an
amazing broccoli & cheese
soup. Now that I'm a stay-at-
home dad, I tried to recreate
it...I think my version is
better than the original!

Just Perfect Sloppy Joes

3 lbs. ground beef, browned
  and drained
1 onion, finely chopped
1 green pepper, chopped
28-oz. can tomato sauce
3/4 c. catsup
3 T. Worcestershire sauce
1 t. chili powder
1/2 t. pepper
1/2 t. garlic powder
8 sandwich buns, split

Combine all ingredients except buns
in a slow cooker. Cover and cook on
low setting for 8 to 10 hours, or on
high setting for 3 to 4 hours. Serve in
sandwich buns. Serves 8.

Amy Wrightsel
Louisville, KY

This recipe brings back
memories of my aunt and me
puttering around in the
kitchen trying to figure
out how to make these
Joe's just perfect.

Roasted Tomato-Feta Broccoli

2 T. olive oil
2 c. broccoli flowerets
1 c. cherry tomatoes
1 t. lemon juice
dried parsley, salt and pepper
   to taste
1/2 c. crumbled feta cheese
Optional: additional olive oil

Heat oil in a skillet over medium
heat. Add broccoli, tomatoes, lemon
juice and seasonings; cook until
vegetables are crisp-tender. Transfer
warm vegetable mixture to a large
bowl and mix in cheese. Drizzle
with additional olive oil, if desired.
Serves 2 to 4.

45

Lyuba Brooke
Jacksonville, FL

This is such a simple and
fast side. Don't let the
easiness of it fool you...
this dish is full of flavor
and it's really healthy.

Cow-Country Beans

3 c. dried red beans
1 lb. cooked ham, cubed
1 onion, sliced
1 c. celery, diced
8-oz. can tomato sauce
2 T. bacon bits
2 T. chili powder
1 T. brown sugar, packed
2 t. garlic powder
1/2 t. smoke-flavored cooking
    sauce
1/2 t. salt

Cover dried beans with water in a bowl; soak overnight. Drain beans; combine with remaining ingredients in a slow cooker. Cover and cook on high setting for 8 to 10 hours. Makes 8 to 10 servings.

Debra Crisp
Grants Pass, OR
My family especially likes these yummy slow-cooker beans served over freshly made potato pancakes.

BBQ Pork Ribs

3 qts. water
4 lbs. pork ribs, cut into
    serving-size portions
1 onion, quartered
2 t. salt
1/4 t. pepper

Bring water to a boil in a large
stockpot. Add ribs, onion, salt and
pepper. Reduce heat; cover and
simmer for 1-1/2 hours. Remove
ribs from pot; drain. Grill ribs for
10 minutes on each side, brushing
frequently with BBQ Sauce, until
tender. Serves 4 to 6.

BBQ Sauce:

1/2 c. vinegar
1 T. lemon juice
1/2 c. chili sauce
1/4 c. Worcestershire sauce
2 T. onion, chopped
1/2 c. brown sugar, packed
1/2 t. dry mustard
1/8 t. garlic powder
1/8 t. cayenne pepper

Combine all ingredients in a
small saucepan. Simmer over
low heat for one hour, stirring
frequently.

47

Diane Gregori
Riverside, CA

A big platter of corn on the
cob is the perfect partner
for these juicy ribs.

Grandma's Buttery Mashed Potatoes

6 to 8 potatoes, peeled and cubed
1/2 c. butter, softened
1 c. evaporated milk
salt and pepper to taste
Garnish: additional butter,
   fresh chives

Cover potatoes with water in a large
saucepan; bring to a boil over
medium-high heat. Cook until
tender, about 15 minutes; drain.
Add remaining ingredients. Beat
with an electric mixer on medium
speed until blended and creamy.
Serves 8 to 12. Garnish as desired.

J.J. Presley
Portland, TX
Grandma used to make these
mashed potatoes every Sunday
for lunch no matter what the
main course was. I can still
taste them to this day!

Paprika Chicken

2 T. oil
3 to 4 lbs. chicken
salt and pepper to taste
1 onion, chopped
1 clove garlic, minced
1 tomato, chopped
1 green pepper, chopped
1-1/2 T. paprika
1/2 c. water
1 c. sour cream
1 T. all-purpose flour
cooked wide egg noodles

Heat oil in a large skillet over medium heat. Season chicken pieces with salt and pepper. Cook chicken in oil until golden, about 7 minutes per side. Remove chicken from pan; drain, reserving 1/4 of drippings in pan. Sauté onion and garlic in drippings until onion is translucent. Stir in tomato, green pepper, paprika and water. Return chicken to skillet; cover and simmer for 35 to 45 minutes. Remove chicken from skillet; set aside. Skim any excess fat from the top. Mix together sour cream and flour; stir into tomato mixture. Stirring constantly, bring mixture to a boil. To serve, top noodles with chicken and ladle sauce over top. Serves 4 to 6.

49

Staci Prickett
Montezuma, GA

This is old Polish comfort food at its finest. One bite, and it'll warm you up from your head to your toes.

Maple-Glazed Carrots

4-1/2 c. water
4 lbs. carrots, peeled and sliced
10 T. butter, divided
6 T. brown sugar, packed
  and divided
1-1/2 t. salt
6 T. maple syrup
Garnish: snipped fresh chives

Bring water to a boil in a large
saucepan over medium-high heat.
Add carrots, 4 tablespoons butter,
3 tablespoons brown sugar and salt.
Reduce heat to medium-low. Cover
and simmer just until carrots are
tender when pierced with a fork,
about 10 minutes. Drain and set
aside. Melt remaining butter in a
large skillet over medium-high heat.
Add maple syrup and remaining
brown sugar; cook and stir until
sugar has dissolved. Reduce heat to
medium-low. Add carrots to syrup
mixture and toss gently. Cook for
5 minutes, or until carrots are evenly
coated and mixture is bubbly.
Sprinkle with chives just before
serving. Serves 10.

Andrea Heyart
Aubrey, TX

These sweet and savory
carrots are a perfect
addition to your family's
table or a fun potluck!

Maple Pork Chops

1/2 c. maple syrup
3 T. soy sauce
2 cloves garlic, minced
4 pork chops

In a bowl, whisk together syrup, soy sauce and garlic; reserve 1/4 cup of mixture. Add pork chops to remaining mixture in bowl. Cover and refrigerate for at least 15 minutes to overnight. Drain, discarding mixture in bowl. Grill over medium-hot heat until browned and cooked through, about 6 minutes per side. Drizzle pork chops with reserved syrup mixture before serving. Makes 4 servings.

51

Emma Brown
Saskatchewan, Canada

The sweetness of the maple syrup and saltiness of the soy sauce go so well together. My family can't get enough of these...I usually have to double the recipe!

Marvelous Mexican Meatloaf

2 lbs. lean ground beef
2 c. tortilla chips, crushed
16-oz. can chili beans
10-oz. can diced tomatoes with
  green chiles, drained
1-1/2 t. chili powder
1/2 t. ground cumin
1 onion, chopped
2 eggs, beaten
1/2 t. salt
1/2 t. pepper

Combine all ingredients in a large
bowl; mix well. Form into a loaf and
place into a lightly greased 9"x5" loaf
pan. Bake, uncovered, at 350 degrees
for 40 minutes, or until meatloaf is
cooked through. Allow meatloaf to
stand 10 minutes before slicing.
Serves 8.

Beckie Apple
Grannis, AR
This quick & easy meatloaf
is a family favorite. It
travels well for potluck
dinners too.

Saucy Limas

2 10-oz. pkgs. frozen baby
  lima beans
1/4 c. molasses
1 T. mustard
1 T. vinegar
1/2 c. catsup
1/8 t. Worcestershire sauce
1/8 t. hot pepper sauce

Cook beans in a saucepan according to package directions; drain. Combine beans with remaining ingredients in saucepan over medium-low heat. Simmer for 5 to 10 minutes, until heated through. Serves 6.

53

Jo Ann
These are some of the best lima beans I've ever had! They've got a tangy kick to them that will have you coming back for more.

Cayenne Fried Chicken

4 boneless, skinless chicken
    breasts
2-1/2 c. milk
2 T. plus 4 drops hot pepper
    sauce
1 t. salt
3/4 c. all-purpose flour, divided
3/4 c. butter, melted
6 T. oil
1/2 t. garlic powder
1 t. fresh chives, chopped
salt and pepper to taste

Place chicken in a deep bowl. Cover with milk; add 2 tablespoons hot sauce and salt. Let stand for one hour. Remove chicken and coat with 6 tablespoons flour; set milk mixture aside. Heat 1/3 cup butter and oil in a large skillet. Cook chicken in butter mixture until browned on both sides and no longer pink in the middle; set aside. Drain skillet, reserving 3 tablespoons drippings in skillet. Add remaining butter and flour; stir until browned. Pour reserved milk into skillet. Add garlic powder, chives, remaining hot sauce, salt and pepper to taste. Bring to a boil; cook and stir until slightly thickened, about 10 minutes. Spoon sauce over chicken before serving. Serves 4.

Vickie
Warm up with this hot & spicy version of classic fried chicken...we guarantee you'll come back for seconds after your mouth cools off!

Shrimp Creole

1/3 c. shortening
1/4 c. all-purpose flour
2 lbs. uncooked large shrimp, peeled and cleaned
1 c. hot water
2 8-oz. cans tomato sauce
1/2 c. green onion, chopped
4 cloves garlic, minced
1/2 c. fresh parsley, chopped
1/4 c. green pepper, chopped
1 slice lemon
2 T. sugar
1-1/2 t. salt
1/2 t. dried thyme
1/8 t. red pepper flakes
2 bay leaves
cooked rice

Melt shortening in a large stockpot over medium heat. Whisk in flour; cook until it starts to brown. Add remaining ingredients except cooked rice. Cover and simmer for 20 minutes. Discard bay leaves. Spoon over cooked rice. Serves 4 to 6.

55

Jill Heilman
Gilbertsville, PA
This recipe was passed down to me from my mom, and I always serve it when I entertain...everyone loves it!

Lighter-Than-Air Potato Rolls

1/2 c. instant mashed potato
    flakes
1 t. sugar
2 T. butter, softened
1/2 c. hot water
1/3 c. cold water
2 c. biscuit baking mix

In a bowl, stir together potato flakes, sugar, butter and hot water. Add cold water and baking mix; stir until a soft dough forms. Gently form dough into a ball on a floured surface; knead 8 to 10 times. Roll out into a 10-inch by 6-inch rectangle. Cut into 12 squares; arrange on an ungreased baking sheet. Bake at 450 degrees for about 10 minutes, or until golden. Makes one dozen.

Linda Cuellar
Riverside, CA

These are wonderful right out of the oven served with butter, jam, apple butter or honey.

Farmhouse Pot Roast

3-lb. beef chuck roast
4-oz. can sliced mushrooms,
   drained
8 redskin potatoes, cubed
1/2 lb. baby carrots
3 stalks celery, chopped
14-1/2 oz. can beef broth
2 c. water
26-oz. can cream of mushroom
   soup

Place roast in a large slow cooker;
top with vegetables. In a bowl, blend
together broth, water and soup; pour
over roast. Cover and cook on low
setting for 6 to 8 hours, until roast
is very tender. Makes 6 servings.

57

Cherylann Smith
Hillsborough, NC

After all day in the slow
cooker, this roast is
falling-apart tender and
makes its own gravy.

Family's Favorite Lasagna

1 lb. ground beef
1/2 c. onion, chopped
6-oz. can tomato paste
28-oz. can diced tomatoes
1-1/2 t. dried oregano
1-1/4 t. garlic powder
1 t. salt
3/4 t. pepper
8-oz. pkg. lasagna noodles,
   cooked
8-oz. pkg. shredded mozzarella
   cheese
12-oz. container cottage cheese
Garnish: grated Parmesan cheese

Brown beef and onion in a large skillet over medium heat; drain. Add tomato paste, tomatoes with juice and seasonings; reduce heat and simmer for 20 minutes. In a greased 11"x7" baking pan, layer half each of lasagna noodles, mozzarella cheese, cottage cheese and meat sauce. Repeat layers, ending with sauce; sprinkle with Parmesan cheese. Bake at 350 degrees for 30 minutes. Let stand several minutes; cut into squares to serve. Makes 6 to 8 servings.

Jo Anne Hayon
Sheboygan, WI

My husband says this lasagna is the best! I've been making it ever since we were married in 1977.

Bacon Florentine Fettuccine

16-oz. pkg. fettuccine pasta,
   uncooked
2 10-oz. pkgs. frozen creamed
   spinach
1/2 lb. bacon, crisply cooked
   and crumbled
1/8 t. garlic powder
1/2 c. plus 2 T. grated Parmesan
   cheese, divided
pepper to taste

Prepare fettuccine in a stockpot as
package directs; drain, reserving
3/4 cup of cooking liquid. Microwave
spinach as directed on package. Add
spinach, bacon and garlic powder to
stockpot. Slowly drizzle reserved
liquid into stockpot until sauce
reaches desired consistency. Return
pasta to stockpot and heat through.
Transfer to a serving dish and stir in
1/2 cup cheese. Season with pepper;
sprinkle with remaining cheese.
Makes 4 servings.

59

Barbara Adamson
Oviedo, FL
This incredibly tasty and
simple pasta dish is
so fast to prepare.

Slow-Cooker Chicken & Dumplings

4 boneless, skinless chicken
  breasts, cubed
2 10-3/4 oz. cans cream of
  chicken soup
2 c. water
1/4 c. onion, finely diced
1 cube chicken bouillon
2 10-oz pkgs. refrigerated
  biscuits, torn into one-inch
  pieces

Combine all ingredients except
biscuits in a slow cooker. Cover and
cook on low setting for 5 to 6 hours.
Thirty minutes before serving, add
biscuit pieces to slow cooker; stir
gently. Cover and cook on high
setting for an additional 30 minutes,
or until biscuits are cooked through.
Serves 4 to 6.

Nicki Slowbe
Cleveland, OH

There's nothing better than
coming home from a long,
hard day to a big helping of
chicken & dumplings. It just
fills you up and makes
you feel sooo good.

Green Bean Bundles

3 14-1/2 oz. cans whole green
   beans, drained
8 slices bacon, cut in half
   crosswise
6 T. butter, melted
1/2 c. brown sugar, packed
2 to 3 cloves garlic, minced

Gather beans in bundles of 10;
wrap each bundle with a half-slice
of bacon. Arrange bundles, seam-
side down, in a lightly greased
13"x9" baking pan. Mix melted
butter, brown sugar and garlic in
a small bowl; spoon over bundles.
Cover and bake at 375 degrees for
30 minutes. Uncover; bake an
additional 15 minutes. Serves 6.

61

Wendy Sensing
Brentwood, TN

Easy and delicious! This is
one of our favorite side
dishes to bring to church
get-togethers...the dish
always comes home empty.

Pulled Pork Barbecue

14-oz. can beef broth
1/2 c. beer or non-alcoholic beer
3 to 4-lb. Boston butt pork roast
18-oz. bottle smoke-flavored
   barbecue sauce
sandwich buns, split

Pour broth and beer into a large slow cooker; add roast. Cover and cook on high setting for 4 hours, or on low setting for 8 hours, until roast is very tender. Remove roast from slow cooker. Shred roast with 2 forks and transfer to a roasting pan. Stir in barbecue sauce. Bake, uncovered, at 350 degrees for 30 minutes. Fill buns with pulled pork to make sandwiches. Makes 10 to 12 servings.

Melanie Foster
North Wilkesboro, NC

This is a budget-friendly, family-pleasing main dish that is requested often in my home. Great served with a side of slaw and baked beans.

Brats, Taters & Apples

5 to 6 bratwurst pork sausage
   links, sliced
5 potatoes, peeled and cubed
27-oz. pkg. sauerkraut, drained
   and rinsed
1 tart apple, cored and chopped
1 onion, chopped
1/4 c. brown sugar, packed

In a skillet over medium heat, brown
bratwurst on all sides. Combine
remaining ingredients in a slow
cooker. Stir in bratwurst and pan
drippings; cover and cook on high
setting for 4 to 6 hours, until
potatoes and apples are tender.
Serves 6.

63

Diane Cohen
The Woodlands, TX

The taste combination of
bratwurst, potatoes and
apples is something special
indeed. It may sound strange,
but one bite and you'll
be a believer.

Sweet Potato Casserole

4 c. mashed sweet potatoes
1/3 c. plus 2 T. butter, melted
   and divided
2 T. sugar
2 eggs, beaten
1/2 c. milk
1/3 c. chopped pecans
1/3 c. sweetened flaked coconut
1/3 c. brown sugar, packed
2 T. all-purpose flour

In a large bowl, mix together sweet potatoes, 1/3 cup butter and sugar. Stir in eggs and milk. Spoon mixture into a lightly greased 2-quart casserole dish. In a separate bowl, combine remaining butter and other ingredients. Sprinkle mixture over sweet potatoes. Bake, uncovered, at 325 degrees for one hour, or until heated through and bubbly. Serves 4.

Dawn Romero
Lewisville, TX

This is great to take to holiday parties or gatherings.

Vermont Maple Chicken

1/4 c. all-purpose flour
salt and pepper to taste
4 boneless, skinless chicken
   breasts
2 T. butter
1/2 c. maple syrup
1 t. dried sage
1/2 t. dried thyme
1/4 t. dried marjoram
1 Spanish onion, sliced
1/2 c. water

65

Place flour, salt and pepper in a large plastic zipping bag. Add chicken to bag and shake to coat evenly; set aside. Melt butter in an oven-safe skillet over medium-high heat. Cook chicken in butter until lightly browned on both sides. Remove skillet from heat. Drizzle syrup over chicken, turning to coat completely. Sprinkle chicken with herbs; place onion slices on top to cover chicken. Add water to skillet. Bake, uncovered, at 350 degrees for 30 minutes. Turn chicken over; bake for an additional 15 to 20 minutes, until chicken juices run clear when pierced. Serves 4.

Paula Spadaccini
Shelburne, VT
A delicious old New England farmhouse recipe that I've modernized, making it easier to prepare. Be sure to use pure maple syrup for the best flavor.

Julie's Chicken Pie

4 c. cooked chicken, cubed
10-3/4 oz. can cream of
  chicken soup
10-1/2 oz. can chicken broth
1/2 t. poultry seasoning
16-oz. can sliced carrots, drained
1-1/2 c. all-purpose flour
2 t. baking powder
1-1/2 c. buttermilk
1/2 c. butter, melted

Place chicken in a lightly greased
13"x9" baking pan. Combine soup,
broth and seasoning in a bowl;
spoon over chicken. Arrange carrots
on top. In another bowl, mix
together flour and baking powder;
stir in buttermilk and melted butter.
Spoon over carrots. Bake, uncovered,
at 350 degrees for one hour, or until
bubbly and crust is golden. Serves 6.

Julie Zahn
Syracuse, NE

This pie is a real crowd-
pleaser! Whether served at
a social event or at home,
it always disappears first.

Skillet Chicken with Vegetables & Herbs

2 T. all-purpose flour
1/8 t. pepper
1/8 t. paprika
2 T. olive oil
4 chicken breasts
2 red onions, quartered
1 lb. new potatoes, quartered
8-oz. pkg. baby carrots
1-1/2 c. chicken broth
3 T. lemon juice
1 T. fresh oregano, chopped
Garnish: chopped fresh thyme

67

Combine flour and seasonings in a small bowl. Coat chicken breasts with mixture. Heat oil in a large oven-safe skillet over medium-high heat. Brown chicken on both sides. Remove chicken from skillet; set aside. Add onions and potatoes to skillet; cook 5 minutes. Add carrots, broth, lemon juice and oregano; bring to a boil. Return chicken to skillet. Cover and bake at 350 degrees for 20 minutes. Uncover and bake an additional 15 minutes, or until chicken juices run clear and vegetables are tender. Garnish with thyme. Serves 4.

Geneva Rogers
Gillette, WY

The beauty of this tasty dish is that it all cooks in one pan...no mound of dirty dishes to clean up once supper's over.

Quick & Easy Lemon Bars

16-oz. pkg. angel food cake mix
22-oz. can lemon pie filling
Optional: chopped pecans,
    sweetened flaked coconut

Combine dry cake mix and pie filling
in a large bowl; mix well. Spread in
a greased 15"x10" jelly-roll pan; top
with pecans or coconut, if desired.
Bake at 350 degrees for 30 minutes.
Let cool; cut into bars. Makes
2-1/2 dozen.

Lynda McCormick
Burkburnett, TX

An even simpler way to make a
super-simple dessert. These
tasty treats are perfect for
whipping up to take to bake
sales or potlucks.

Candy Apple Cheesecake

21-oz. can apple pie filling,
   divided
9-inch graham cracker crust
2 8-oz. pkgs. cream cheese,
   softened
1/2 c. sugar
1/2 t. vanilla extract
2 eggs, beaten
1/2 c. caramel ice cream topping
12 pecan halves
2 T. chopped pecans

Reserve 1/2 cup apple pie filling;
spoon remaining filling into crust.
In a bowl, beat together cream
cheese, sugar and vanilla until
smooth. Add eggs and beat well;
pour over filling. Bake at 350 degrees
for 35 minutes, or until center is set;
cool. Combine caramel topping and
reserved apple pie filling in a small
saucepan; cook and stir over medium
heat for about one minute. Spoon
caramel mixture evenly over
cheesecake. Arrange pecan halves
around edge; sprinkle with chopped
pecans. Keep chilled until serving.
Serves 8 to 12.

69

Sherry Gordon
Arlington Heights, IL

My family loves to have a
big slice of this after a
hearty fall meal, but it's
delicious any time of year!

Cranberry & Vanilla Chip Cookies

1/2 c. butter, softened
1-1/3 c. sugar
2 eggs, beaten
1 t. imitation butter flavor
1-3/4 c. all-purpose flour
1 c. long-cooking oats, uncooked
1-1/2 t. baking soda
1/2 t. salt
1 c. sweetened dried cranberries
1 c. white chocolate chips

In a large bowl, beat butter and sugar until light and fluffy. Add eggs and butter flavor; mix well. Add flour, oats, baking soda and salt; mix well. Stir in cranberries and chocolate chips. Drop dough by rounded tablespoonfuls, 2 inches apart, onto greased baking sheets. Bake at 350 degrees for 9 to 11 minutes, until edges are golden. Cool one minute on baking sheets. Remove to wire racks; cool completely. Makes 3 dozen.

Cindy Daniel
Bellbrook, OH

I use one cup of the white chocolate chips because I like to taste them in every cookie.

Blue Goose Pie

2 c. fresh gooseberries
2-1/2 c. fresh blueberries
3/4 c. sugar
1/4 t. salt
1/2 t. cinnamon
1/4 c. cornstarch
2 9-inch pie crusts
1 T. butter, sliced

In a bowl, mix together berries,
sugar, salt, cinnamon and cornstarch;
toss to coat berries well. Line a
9" pie plate with one pie crust.
Pour berry mixture into crust; dot
with butter. Cover with top crust;
seal and vent crust. Bake pie at
450 degrees for 50 minutes, or until
crust is golden and filling is bubbly.
Serves 8.

71

Jean Manahan
Waynesboro, PA
A big, berry-full slice
of this pie and a scoop of
vanilla ice cream is the
best dessert I can imagine!

The Perfect Peanut Brittle

1-1/2 c. sugar
3/4 c. water
1/2 c. light corn syrup
1-1/2 c. raw peanuts
2 T. butter
2-1/4 t. baking soda
1 t. vanilla extract

Combine sugar, water and corn syrup in a heavy saucepan over medium heat. Cook and stir until sugar is dissolved. Increase heat to medium-high. Bring to a boil; boil until mixture reaches the thread stage, or 230 to 233 degrees on a candy thermometer. Add peanuts. Cook, stirring often, until mixture reaches the hard-crack stage, or 290 to 310 degrees on a candy thermometer. Remove from heat; stir in butter, baking soda and vanilla. Pour into a greased rimmed baking sheet. Tilt pan back and forth until mixture evenly coats the bottom of the pan. Cool completely. Break into small pieces; store in an airtight container. Makes about 4 cups.

Jennifer Niemi
Nova Scotia, Canada

My best friend lives a long way away. Every year I send her some of this yummy brittle...she says it's her favorite!

Black Forest Brownie Sundaes

18-oz. pkg. brownie mix
21-oz. can cherry pie filling,
    divided
1/4 c. oil
2 eggs, beaten
1-1/4 c. semi-sweet chocolate
    chips
Garnish: vanilla ice cream

In a large bowl, mix together dry
brownie mix, one cup pie filling,
oil and eggs. Pour into a greased
13"x9" baking pan. Bake at
350 degrees for 30 to 35 minutes,
until firm. Sprinkle hot brownies
with chocolate chips; spread chips
with a knife when melted. Let cool;
cut into squares. Top servings with
a scoop of ice cream and some of the
remaining pie filling. Serves 8 to 12.

73

Sheila Murray
Tehachapi, CA

I love to make these for
Valentine's Day, but they're
good anytime of the year...
plus they're very easy!

Blue Pan Cranberry Cake

1 c. fresh cranberries
3/4 c. sugar, divided
1/4 c. chopped walnuts
1 egg
1/2 c. all-purpose flour
6 T. butter, melted
Garnish: whipped cream or
   ice cream

Spread cranberries in a greased
9" pie plate. Sprinkle cranberries
with 1/4 cup sugar and walnuts; set
aside. In a bowl, beat together egg
and remaining sugar. Add flour and
melted butter; beat well and pour
over cranberries. Bake at 325 degrees
for 40 to 45 minutes, until golden
on top. Garnish as desired. Serves 8.

Karen Urfer
New Philadelphia, OH
A warm, country-style cake
I always bake in my blue
spongeware pie pan.

Super Berry Crisp

21-oz. can cherry pie filling
2 c. fresh blueberries
1/4 c. butter
1/3 c. long-cooking oats,
   uncooked
1/3 c. all-purpose flour
1/4 c. brown sugar, packed
1 t. sugar
1/4 t. cinnamon
Garnish: whipped cream

Pour pie filling into an ungreased
9" pie plate; fold in blueberries.
Melt butter in a small saucepan over
medium-low heat. Add remaining
ingredients except garnish to melted
butter, stirring to coat well. Spread
oat mixture over fruit in pie plate.
Bake at 350 degrees for 35 minutes,
or until topping is crisp and golden.
Garnish individual servings with
whipped cream. Serves 8.

Sandy Widdows
Tucson, AZ
I made this recipe one day
with only the ingredients I
had on hand. It turned out
to be one of my husband's
favorites...now I make it
all the time!

Angel Strudel

1 c. butter
2 c. all-purpose flour
3 egg yolks
2 T. vinegar
1/4 c. water
1 c. walnuts, ground
1 c. maraschino cherries,
   chopped
18-1/4 oz. pkg. angel food
   cake mix

In a large bowl, cut butter into flour until mixture resembles coarse crumbs; set aside. In a separate bowl, whisk together egg yolks, vinegar and water; add to butter mixture and mix well. Divide dough into 4 portions; cover and refrigerate 8 hours to overnight. When ready to prepare strudel, roll out one portion of dough into a very thin rectangle. In a bowl, combine walnuts, cherries and dry cake mix; divide into 4 equal portions. Spread one quarter of the filling on rolled dough. Roll up, starting at one short edge. Repeat with remaining 3 portions of dough and filling. Place each on an ungreased baking sheet. Bake each strudel at 325 degrees for 25 minutes. Slice to serve. Makes 4 strudels; each serves 8 to 10.

Jo Baker
Litchfield, IL

This is one of my favorite recipes from my grandmother's farm home, where we kept busy from morning until night.

Cinnamon Poached Pears

4 pears
1 c. pear nectar
1 c. water
3/4 c. maple syrup
2 4-inch cinnamon sticks,
   slightly crushed
4 strips lemon zest

Peel and core pears from the bottom, leaving stems intact. Cut a thin slice off bottom so pears will stand up; set aside. Combine remaining ingredients in a saucepan. Bring to a boil over medium heat, stirring occasionally. Add pears, standing right-side up. Reduce heat and simmer, covered, for 20 to 30 minutes, until tender. Remove pears from pan. Continue to simmer sauce in pan until reduced to 3/4 cup, about 15 minutes. Serve pears drizzled with sauce. Serves 4.

77

Melanie Lowe
Dover, DE
A light dessert that's not too sweet, or serve as a delicious side dish for roast chicken.

Wild Blueberry Gingerbread

2-1/2 c. all-purpose flour
1 c. sugar
1/2 t. ground cloves
1/2 t. cinnamon
1/2 t. ground ginger
1 t. salt
1 t. baking soda
1/2 c. molasses
2 eggs, beaten
1/2 c. oil
1 c. hot tea
1 c. fresh blueberries
Garnish: whipped cream

In a large bowl, mix together flour, sugar, spices and baking soda. Stir in molasses, eggs, oil and tea. Carefully fold in blueberries. Spoon batter into a greased and floured 13"x9" baking pan. Bake at 350 degrees for about 35 minutes, until a toothpick inserted in the center tests clean. Cool; cut into squares and top with a dollop of whipped cream. Makes 13 to 15 servings.

Gail Hageman
Albion, ME

Because it's a twist on an old favorite, this gingerbread is always popular when I take it to a potluck dinner.

Strawberry-Rhubarb Pie

1 c. plus 1 T. sugar, divided
1/3 c. all-purpose flour
2 9-inch pie crusts
2 c. strawberries, hulled, sliced
   and divided
2 c. rhubarb, chopped and
   divided
2 T. butter, sliced

In a bowl, mix together one cup sugar and flour; set aside. Line a 9" pie plate with one unbaked crust. Spoon one cup strawberries and one cup rhubarb into crust. Sprinkle half of sugar mixture over fruit in crust. Repeat layers with remaining strawberries, rhubarb and sugar mixture; dot with butter. Cover with top crust; seal edges and cut 3 slits in the top to vent. Cover edge of crust with strips of aluminum foil. Bake at 425 degrees for 40 to 50 minutes, until golden, removing foil 15 minutes before pie is done. Serves 8.

79

Sarah Putnam
Boonville, IN
I got this recipe from a friend and my whole family loves it...even my kids who are rather hesitant to try new things!

Cinnamon Gingersnaps

3/4 c. butter, softened
1 c. brown sugar, packed
1 egg, beaten
1/4 c. molasses
2-1/4 c. all-purpose flour
2 t. baking soda
1/2 t. salt
2 t. cinnamon
1 t. ground ginger
1/2 to 1 c. sugar

Blend together butter and brown sugar in a large bowl. Mix in egg and molasses; set aside. In a separate bowl, combine flour, baking soda, salt, cinnamon and ginger. Gradually add flour mixture to butter mixture; mix well. Roll dough into one-inch balls; roll in sugar. Arrange 2 inches apart on ungreased baking sheets. Bake at 350 degrees for 10 to 12 minutes, until cookies are set and tops are cracked. Remove to wire racks; cool completely. Makes 4 dozen.

Lisa Ashton
Aston, PA
These spicy-sweet cookies are so nice for dipping into a cup of warm, calming herbal tea.

Chocolate-Raspberry Brownies

1 c. butter
5 1-oz. sqs. unsweetened baking
   chocolate, chopped
2 c. sugar
4 eggs, beaten
2 t. vanilla extract
1-1/4 c. all-purpose flour
1 t. baking powder
1/2 t. salt
1 c. chopped walnuts, toasted
1/2 c. raspberry preserves

Melt butter and chocolate in a heavy saucepan over low heat, stirring constantly, until smooth. Remove from heat. Whisk in sugar, eggs and vanilla. In a small bowl, mix flour, baking powder and salt. Add to chocolate mixture and whisk to blend. Stir in nuts. Pour 2 cups batter into a greased 13"x9" baking pan. Freeze until firm, about 20 minutes. Spread preserves over frozen batter in pan; spoon remaining batter over preserves. Let stand 20 minutes to thaw. Bake at 350 degrees for about 35 minutes, or until a toothpick tests clean. Cut into squares; transfer to a wire rack to cool. Makes about 2 dozen.

Susan Brzozowski
Ellicott City, MD

The layer of raspberries makes these brownies really special!

Peanut Butter Apple Crisp

1 c. all-purpose flour
1-1/2 c. brown sugar, packed
1 t. cinnamon
3/4 c. creamy peanut butter
1/3 c. butter, softened
6 to 8 tart apples, peeled, cored
   and thinly sliced
2 T. lemon juice
1 t. lemon zest
Garnish: vanilla ice cream

Combine flour, brown sugar and
cinnamon in a bowl. Cut in peanut
butter and butter until mixture
resembles coarse crumbs; set aside.
Arrange apple slices in a lightly
greased 13"x9" baking pan; sprinkle
with lemon juice and zest. Top
apples with crumb mixture. Bake at
350 degrees for 35 to 45 minutes.
Serve warm, topped with a scoop of
ice cream. Serves 10 to 12.

Linda Belon
Wintersville, OH
Scrumptious served warm,
topped with generous scoops
of smooth vanilla ice cream.

Coconut Cream Pie

3/4 c. sugar, divided
1/2 t. salt
3 T. cornstarch
2-1/2 c. whole milk
3 eggs, separated
1 t. vanilla extract
1 T. butter, melted
3/4 c. sweetened flaked coconut
9-inch pie crust, baked

In a saucepan over medium-low heat, combine 1/2 cup sugar, salt, cornstarch and milk. Cook until slightly thickened. Place egg yolks in a bowl. Pour 1/4 cup of milk mixture into yolks; beat until well combined. Transfer yolk mixture back to milk mixture; cook and stir for about 2 minutes, until thickened. Stir in vanilla, butter and coconut; pour into pie crust. Set aside to cool. In a bowl, beat together egg whites and remaining sugar with an electric mixer on high speed until stiff peaks form. Top cooled pie with egg white mixture. Bake at 425 degrees for about 5 minutes, until meringue is golden. Serves 8.

Eleanor Dionne
Beverly, MA

Spreading meringue so it touches the edges of the pie crust is the secret to keep it from shrinking...works every time!

Butter Pecan Ice Cream

2 c. whipping cream
14-oz. can sweetened condensed milk
1 to 1-1/2 c. chopped pecans, toasted
3 T. butter, melted
1 t. maple extract

In a large bowl, beat cream with an electric mixer on high setting until stiff peaks form. Combine remaining ingredients in a separate bowl; mix well. Gently fold condensed milk mixture into whipped cream. Pour into a 9"x5" loaf pan. Cover and freeze for at least 6 hours, until firm. Store in freezer until ready to serve. Makes about 2 quarts.

Jennie Gist
Gooseberry Patch

Nothing's better than a big bowl of butter pecan ice cream on a hot summer day!

Root Beer Cake

1 c. sugar
1/2 c. butter, softened
1/2 t. vanilla extract
2 eggs, beaten
2 c. all-purpose flour
1 T. baking powder
1 t. salt
2/3 c. root beer

Combine all ingredients in a large bowl. Blend with an electric mixer on low speed; beat for 3 minutes on medium speed. Pour into a greased and floured 8"x8" baking pan. Bake at 375 degrees for 30 to 35 minutes, until a toothpick tests clean. Spread Frosting over cooled cake. Serves 8 to 10.

Frosting:

1/4 c. butter
1/8 t. salt
2 c. powdered sugar
2 to 4 T. milk
1/3 c. root beer, chilled

In a bowl, beat together all ingredients except root beer. Add root beer; beat to desired consistency.

Tish DeYoung
Wausau, WI

Yes, this cake may sound unusual, but it's wonderful!

Apple-Pear Pie

2 to 3 apples, peeled, cored
and sliced
29-oz. can sliced pears
1 T. all-purpose flour
1/4 c. brown sugar, packed
1 T. cinnamon
2 9-inch pie crusts

Place apples and undrained pears in
a large bowl. Add flour, brown sugar
and cinnamon; stir to mix well. Line
a 9" pie plate with one unbaked pie
crust. Spoon fruit mixture into pie
crust. Top with remaining pie crust
and crimp edges. Cut 3 slits to vent.
Bake at 400 degrees for 10 minutes.
Lower heat to 325 degrees; bake for
an additional 40 minutes, or until
crust is golden. Serves 8.

Molly Ebert
Decatur, IN

So easy to put together.
This is an autumn favorite
at my house.

Hucklebucks

3/4 c. shortening
2 eggs, beaten
3/4 c. baking cocoa
1-1/2 c. sugar
3 t. vanilla extract, divided
1-1/2 c. all-purpose flour
1 T. baking powder
3/4 t. plus 1/8 t. salt, divided
1-1/2 c. plus 1 T. milk, divided
3/4 c. butter, softened
2 c. powdered sugar
1 c. marshmallow creme

In a large bowl, beat together shortening, eggs, cocoa, sugar and 1-1/2 teaspoon vanilla. In a separate bowl, sift together flour, baking powder and 3/4 teaspoon salt. Add 1-1/2 cups milk to cocoa mixture, alternating with dry ingredients. Mix well after each addition until batter is smooth. Drop by tablespoonfuls onto ungreased baking sheets. Bake at 400 degrees for 7 to 8 minutes; cool. Blend together remaining vanilla, salt, milk and other ingredients; spread on one side of a cookie and top with a second cookie. Repeat with remaining cookies. Makes 2 dozen.

Shannon Ellis
Mount Vernon, WA

Soft chocolate cookies with a marshmallow filling... everybody I know loves these tasty treats!

Double Peanut Cookies

1 c. all-purpose flour
1/2 t. baking soda
1/2 c. shortening
1/2 c. creamy peanut butter
1/2 c. sugar
1/2 c. brown sugar, packed
1 egg, beaten
1/2 c. salted dry-roasted peanuts

In a bowl, mix together flour and baking soda; set aside. In a separate large bowl, beat shortening and peanut butter until well blended. Add sugars; beat until fluffy. Beat in egg. Stir in flour mixture until well blended; stir in peanuts. Drop by rounded teaspoonfuls, 2 inches apart, onto ungreased baking sheets; flatten slightly. Bake at 350 degrees for 10 to 12 minutes, until lightly golden. Cool on baking sheets for about 5 minutes; remove to a wire rack to cool completely. Makes 3 dozen.

Jo Ann
For all the peanut lovers out there! Smooth peanut cookies with crunchy roasted peanuts...too good.

Luscious Angel Cupcakes

16-oz. pkg. angel food cake mix
3.4-oz. pkg instant vanilla
    pudding mix
2 8-oz. cans crushed pineapple
1 c. frozen whipped topping,
    thawed
2 c. assorted fresh berries

Prepare cake mix as directed on the
package. Pour batter into 24 to
30 paper-lined muffin cups, filling
each 2/3 full. Bake at 375 degrees
for 12 to 15 minutes, until tops are
golden and a toothpick tests clean.
Cool cupcakes in pan for 10 minutes;
remove to wire racks to cool
completely. In a bowl, mix together
dry pudding mix and undrained
pineapple. Gently fold in whipped
topping; spread evenly over cupcakes.
Top each cupcake with berries; store
in refrigerator until ready to serve.
Makes 2 to 2-1/2 dozen.

Sandra Sullivan
Aurora, CO

These are our favorite
summer birthday treats...
they're great to take
to picnics or to a
poolside party.

Chocolate Scotcheroos

1 c. sugar
1 c. light corn syrup
1 c. creamy peanut butter
6 c. crispy rice cereal
1 c. semi-sweet chocolate chips
1 c. butterscotch chips

In a large saucepan over medium heat, combine sugar and corn syrup; heat until bubbling. Remove from heat; stir in peanut butter until well blended. Add cereal and mix until well coated. Press into a greased 13"x9" baking pan; let cool. Combine chips in a microwave-safe bowl. Microwave on high setting for one to 2 minutes, stirring after one minute, until melted. Spread melted chips evenly over cereal mixture; let stand until firm. Cut into bars. Makes 20 to 24 bars.

Mary Haynes
Blue Mountain, MS

I have been making these for more than 40 years. I made them for my sisters before I married, and now my own children and grandchildren love them!

Poppy Seed Cake

18-1/4 oz. pkg. yellow cake mix
1 c. oil
1 c. sour cream
1/2 c. sugar
4 eggs, beaten
1/4 c. poppy seed

In a large bowl, beat together dry cake mix and all remaining ingredients. Pour into a greased and floured Bundt® pan. Bake at 325 degrees for one hour, or until a toothpick inserted tests clean. Turn cake out onto a serving plate. Drizzle Glaze over top. Serves 8 to 10.

Glaze:

1/2 c. sugar
1/4 c. orange juice
1/2 t. almond extract
1/2 t. imitation butter flavor
1/2 t. vanilla extract

Combine all ingredients; mix well.

Holly Curry
Middleburgh, NY
The glaze drizzled over this simple cake sets it apart from other poppy seed cakes.

Garlic Dill Pickles

9 c. pickling cucumbers, sliced
3 1-quart canning jars and lids,
  sterilized
3 grape leaves
3 t. dill seed
3 cloves garlic
6 c. white vinegar
3 qts. water
1-1/2 c. salt

Pack cucumbers evenly between sterilized jars, leaving 1/2-inch headspace. To each jar add one grape leaf, one teaspoon dill seed and one clove garlic. Combine remaining ingredients in a large saucepan over medium heat. Cook and stir until hot and salt is dissolved. Pour vinegar evenly into hot sterilized jars, leaving 1/2-inch headspace. Wipe rims; secure with lids and rings. Process in a boiling water bath for 15 minutes; set jars on a towel to cool. Check for seals. Makes 3 jars.

Barbara Lengler
Dover, OH

This is a tasty recipe
I found in an old church
cookbook. They have a great
dill flavor and are
very crunchy.

Old-Time Corncob Jelly

1 doz. corncobs
2 qts. water
1-3/4 oz. pkg. powdered fruit
    pectin
3 c. sugar
5 to 6 1/2-pint canning jars and
    lids, sterilized

In a large stockpot over high heat,
combine corncobs and water. Bring
to a boil; reduce heat to medium-low
and simmer for 35 to 40 minutes.
Discard cobs; strain liquid through
a cheesecloth-lined colander.
Measure 3 cups of liquid into a
large saucepan, adding water if
needed to equal 3 cups. Gradually
dissolve pectin into liquid; bring
to a rolling boil over high heat. Add
sugar all at once, stirring to dissolve.
Return to a rolling boil; boil for
5 minutes, stirring constantly.
Remove from heat; skim foam. Ladle
into hot sterilized jars, leaving
1/4-inch headspace. Wipe rims;
secure with lids and rings. Process in
a boiling-water bath for 10 minutes.
Set jars on a towel to cool; check for
seals. Makes 5 to 6 jars.

93

Dale Duncan
Waterloo, IA

Here in Iowa we eat a lot
of sweet corn, so I was
excited to find something
yummy to make out of stuff
folks usually throw
away...corncobs!

Our Favorite Salsa

2 lbs. tomatoes, peeled and
  chopped
2 c. green peppers, chopped
29-oz. can tomato sauce
2 c. onions, chopped
6 to 12 jalapeño peppers,
  chopped
2 T. chili powder
1 T. dried oregano
1 T. ground cumin
1 T. fresh cilantro, chopped
1 T. garlic powder
1 T. red pepper flakes
1 T. salt
1 T. sugar
10 T. lemon juice
5 1-pint canning jars and lids,
  sterilized

Combine tomatoes and remaining
ingredients except lemon juice in a
large stockpot; bring to a boil over
medium heat. Reduce heat; simmer
for 30 minutes. Add 2 tablespoons
lemon juice to each hot sterilized
jar. Spoon salsa into jars, leaving
1/2-inch headspace. Wipe rims;
secure with lids and rings. Process
for 15 minutes in a boiling water
bath. Set on towels to cool; check
for seals. Makes 4 to 5 jars.

June Eier
Findlay, OH

Nothing compares to fresh,
homemade salsa...you'll
never go back to
store-bought again!

Classic Country Canning
Amish Hot Pepper Rings

2 T. lemon pepper
1 T. salt
1 T. garlic powder
1 T. onion powder
1 c. oil
1 c. olive oil
2 c. white vinegar
2-1/2 c. sugar
12-oz. can tomato paste
12 lbs. green peppers, sliced into
   rings and seeds removed
13 lbs. hot banana peppers,
   sliced into rings and seeds
   removed
8 1-pint canning jars and lids,
   sterilized

95

Combine all ingredients except
peppers in a very large stockpot;
bring to a boil. Turn off heat and
add pepper rings. Set aside for
20 minutes, stirring occasionally.
Spoon into hot sterilized jars,
leaving 1/4-inch headspace. Wipe
rims; secure lids and rings. Process
in a boiling water bath for
20 minutes. Set jars on a towel
to cool. Check for seals.
Makes 8 jars.

Cyndy DeStefano
Mercer, PA

Our Amish neighbor taught
me how to preserve peppers
several different ways,
but this way is by far our
favorite! We enjoy them
on just about everything.

Fresh Herb Pesto Sauce

2 c. fresh herb leaves, coarsely
   chopped
6 cloves garlic, chopped
1 c. nuts, chopped
1/2 c. olive oil
1/2 t. salt
3/4 c. grated Parmesan or
   Romano cheese

Mix herbs, garlic, nuts, 1/2 cup oil
and salt in a blender. Process until
smooth, adding a little more oil if
needed to make blending easier.
Transfer to a bowl and stir in grated
cheese. Refrigerate in an airtight
container, or spoon into ice cube
trays and freeze for later use. Makes
about 1-1/2 cups.

Colleen Hinker
Santa Rosa, NM

Classic pesto is made
with basil and pine nuts,
but try other tasty
combinations, like rosemary
and pecans or oregano and
almonds...delicious!

Tipton Family Spaghetti Sauce

1/2 bushel or 30 lbs. tomatoes,
    peeled, halved and seeded
3 lbs. onions, chopped
1 to 2 c. oil
1/2 c. sugar
1/2 c. canning salt
2 T. dried oregano
2 T. dried basil
Optional: minced garlic and
    sweet & hot peppers to taste
4 12-oz. cans tomato paste
20 T. lemon juice
10 1-quart canning jars and lids,
    sterilized

In a large stockpot, mix together all
ingredients except tomato paste.
Bring to a boil over medium heat.
Reduce heat to low; simmer for one
hour. Add tomato paste; return to a
boil. Add 2 tablespoons lemon juice
to each hot sterilized jar. Spoon sauce
into jars, leaving 1/4-inch headspace.
Wipe rims; secure with lids and rings.
Process in a boiling water bath for
40 minutes. Set jars on a towel to
cool completely; check for seals.
Makes 9 to 10 jars.

Doris Tipton
Green Mountain, NC
Now that my daughters are
grown, we get together in
the summer and prepare this
sauce to can...we have a
wonderful time together!

Ruby's Pickled Eggs

1 c. brown sugar, packed
1 c. cider vinegar
1 qt. pickled beets
15 to 20 whole cloves
Optional: 1 to 2 drops red food coloring
1 doz. eggs, hard-boiled and peeled

In a saucepan over medium heat, combine sugar, vinegar, beets with juice, cloves and red food coloring, if using. Heat until very warm, but do not boil. Place eggs in a large glass jar or bowl with a lid. Pour vinegar mixture over eggs. Let cool; cover jar and refrigerate. Will keep in refrigerator for up to a week. Makes 12 servings of beets and eggs.

Deirdre Foltz
Findlay, OH

I received this recipe from a friend of the family many years ago and it has become a favorite. It's easily doubled and a delicious way to use up leftover Easter eggs!

Quick Picnic Pickles

1/2 c. rice vinegar
1/2 c. sugar
1-quart wide-mouth canning jar
   and lid, sterilized
2 cucumbers, peeled and thinly
   sliced
1/2 red, orange or yellow pepper,
   cut into long strips
1/8 red onion, cut into wedges
   or strips
1 carrot, peeled and thinly sliced
1 T. fresh cilantro, chopped

Combine vinegar and sugar in
canning jar. Shake to mix well.
Add vegetables and cilantro to jar in
small layers and pack to top. Fill with
water to cover vegetables. Replace lid;
seal tightly. Turn over jar to mix well.
Refrigerate overnight before using.
May store in refrigerator for up to
one week. Makes one jar.

Lisa Sett
Thousand Oaks, CA

Jars of these fresh veggie
pickles make great gifts
to share with friends
& neighbors.

Gooseberry Conserve

Angie Stone
Argillite, KY

Served with roast chicken or turkey, this conserve is simply divine!

3 lbs. fresh gooseberries
3 lbs. sugar
16-oz. pkg. raisins
juice and zest of 3 oranges
2 c. chopped walnuts
4 1-pint canning jars and lids,
   sterilized

Combine all ingredients except nuts
in a large heavy saucepan. Bring to a
boil over medium heat, stirring until
sugar dissolves. Reduce heat and cook
until thickened, stirring frequently.
Mix in nuts. Spoon into hot
sterilized jars, leaving 1/4-inch
headspace. Wipe rims; secure with
lids and rings. Process in a boiling
water bath for 10 minutes; set jars
on a towel to cool. Check for seals.
Makes 3 to 4 jars.

Aunt Ruth's Dilly Beans

2 lbs. green beans, trimmed
4 1-pint canning jars and lids,
  sterilized
4 sprigs fresh dill
4 cloves garlic, sliced
Optional: 1 t. red pepper flakes
2-1/2 c. white vinegar
2-1/2 c. water
1/4 c. canning salt

Pack beans upright into hot sterilized
jars, leaving 1/2-inch headspace.
Divide dill, garlic and red pepper
flakes, if using, evenly among jars.
Combine remaining ingredients in a
saucepan; bring to a boil. Pour hot
liquid into jars, leaving 1/2-inch
headspace. Remove air bubbles by
gently running a thin plastic spatula
between beans and inside of jars.
Wipe rims; secure with lids and rings.
Process in a boiling water bath for
10 minutes; set jars on a towel to
cool. Check for seals. Makes 4 jars.

Laura Lett
Delaware, OH

My mom, who always had a
tremendous vegetable garden,
passed this recipe along
to me. A side of these
flavorful green beans really
perks up a simple meal!

All-Day Apple Butter

3-1/2 lbs. Pippin apples, peeled,
    cored and sliced
2 lbs. Granny Smith apples,
    peeled, cored and sliced
2 c. sugar
2 c. brown sugar, packed
2 t. cinnamon
1/4 t. ground cloves
1/4 t. salt
1/8 t. nutmeg
6 1/2-pint canning jars and
    lids, sterilized

Place all ingredients in a large slow
cooker. Stir to mix well. Cover and
cook on high setting for one hour.
Reduce heat to low setting and
cook 9 to 11 hours more, stirring
occasionally, until mixture is thick
and dark brown. Uncover; cook one
hour longer. Ladle hot butter into
hot sterilized jars, leaving 1/4-inch
headspace. Wipe rims; secure with
lids and rings. Process in a boiling
water bath for 10 minutes. Set jars
on a towel to cool; check for seals.
Makes 5 to 6 jars.

Cheryl Volbruck
Costa Mesa, CA

A slow-cooker favorite!
One taste of this apple
butter on a warm biscuit
or in a bowl of oatmeal and
you won't be eating any
other apple butter again!

Classic Country Canning
Mom's Peach Butter

18 peaches, peeled, pitted
   and crushed
4 c. sugar
1 t. ground cloves
1/2 t. nutmeg
1/2 t. ground ginger
4 t. cinnamon
4 1-pint canning jars and
   lids, sterilized

Combine crushed peaches and
remaining ingredients in a large
stockpot. Simmer over medium
heat, stirring constantly, until
thickened, about 30 minutes. Ladle
hot mixture into hot sterilized jars,
leaving 1/2-inch headspace. Wipe
rims; secure with lids and rings.
Process in a boiling water bath for
10 minutes. Set jars on a towel to
cool; check for seals. Makes 3 to
4 jars.

103

Violet Leonard
Chesapeake, VA

Growing up, we had a huge
garden and a lot of fruit
trees...this is one of the
many delicious things
Mom canned.

Spiced Blueberry Jam

4-1/2 c. fresh blueberries,
   crushed
1/2 t. cinnamon
1/2 t. ground cloves
7 c. sugar
juice of 1 lemon
3-oz. pkg. liquid fruit pectin
8 1/2-pint canning jars and lids,
   sterilized

Combine blueberries, spices, sugar and lemon juice in a large stockpot. Bring to a boil over medium-high heat, stirring constantly. Boil for 2 minutes; add pectin. Boil again, stirring constantly, for one minute longer. Remove from heat; skim off foam. Spoon into hot sterilized jars, leaving 1/4-inch headspace. Wipe rims; secure with lids and rings. Process in a boiling water bath for 10 minutes. Set jars on a towel to cool completely; check for seals. Makes 7 to 8 jars.

Beth Bennett
Stratham, NH

Whenever my mother made this yummy jam, we used to love to dip small pretzels in it. Now when I make it, I always think of her.

Strawberry-Thyme Jam

4 pts. fresh strawberries, hulled and crushed
1 T. fresh thyme, chopped
1-3/4 oz. pkg. powdered fruit pectin
Optional: 1/2 t. butter
7 c. sugar
8 1/2-pint canning jars and lids, sterilized

Place strawberries into a large stockpot; add thyme. Stir in pectin and mix well. Add butter, if using, to reduce foaming. Bring mixture to a rolling boil over high heat, stirring constantly. Add sugar all at once. Return to a rolling boil; boil for one minute. Remove from heat; skim off foam. Spoon into hot sterilized jars, leaving 1/4-inch headspace. Wipe rims; secure with lids and rings. Process in a boiling water bath for 10 minutes. Set jars on a towel to cool completely; check for seals. Makes 7 to 8 jars.

Sharon Demers
Dolores, CO

I love the taste of strawberries and fresh thyme, and this is a refreshing jam that's oh-so good on buttermilk scones or hot biscuits.

Classic Country Canning
Jalapeño Jelly

8 green peppers, seeded and
   chopped
6 jalapeño peppers, seeded
   and chopped
6 c. sugar
1/2 c. vinegar
6-oz. pkg. liquid fruit pectin
2 to 3 drops green food coloring
6 1/2-pint canning jars and
   lids, sterilized

Place all peppers in a food processor
and process until well minced.
Transfer minced peppers to a
strainer. Press until 2 cups pepper
juice have been collected; discard
pulp. In a large stockpot over
medium-high heat, combine sugar,
vinegar and pepper juice. Bring to a
boil; boil rapidly for 10 minutes. Stir
in pectin and food coloring. Heat,
stirring constantly, until mixture
comes to a rolling boil; boil for
one minute. Remove from heat;
skim off foam. Ladle hot jelly into
hot sterilized jars, leaving 1/4-inch
headspace. Wipe rims; secure with
lids and rings. Process in a boiling
water bath for 10 minutes. Set jars
on a towel to cool; check for seals.
Makes 5 to 6 jars.

Kathe Nych
Mercer, PA

A tasty, sweet-hot jelly...
add more heat by using more
hot peppers. It makes a great
gift in a vintage jar tied
with a big red ribbon!

Jennie's Raspberry Vinegar

1-1/2 c. white vinegar
1/2 c. sugar
1 c. fresh raspberries

Combine vinegar and sugar in a saucepan over medium heat. Heat, stirring occasionally, until hot but not boiling and sugar is dissolved. Pour into a glass bowl; stir in raspberries. Cover with plastic wrap and let stand in a cool place 6 to 7 days. Strain through cheesecloth twice; discard berries. Pour vinegar into sterilized jars or bottles with a tight-fitting lid. May be stored for several months in the refrigerator. Makes 1-1/2 to 2 cups.

Annette Ingram
Grand Rapids, MI

My friend Jennie planted a raspberry patch, and this year she gifted us with bottles of her own flavored vinegar.

INDEX

INDEX

Copy & Cut Canning Labels

Use these labels to add a touch of whimsy to your favorite canned delights!
Duplicate and enlarge on a color copier as needed.

to: _____
from: _____

A little gift from

from the kitchen of:

to:

from:

Our Story

Back in 1984, we were next-door neighbors raising our families in the little town of Delaware, Ohio. Two moms with small children, we were looking for a way to do what we loved and stay home with the kids too. We had always shared a love of home cooking and making memories with family & friends and so, after many a conversation over the backyard fence, **Gooseberry Patch** was born.

We put together our first catalog at our kitchen tables, enlisting the help of our loved ones wherever we could. From that very first mailing, we found an immediate connection with many of our customers and it wasn't long before we began receiving letters, photos and recipes from these new friends. In 1992, we put together our very first cookbook, compiled from hundreds of these recipes and, the rest, as they say, is history.

Hard to believe it's been over 25 years since those kitchen-table days! From that original little **Gooseberry Patch** family, we've grown to include an amazing group of creative folks who love cooking, decorating and creating as much as we do. Today, we're best known for our homestyle, family-friendly cookbooks, now recognized as national bestsellers.

JoAnn & Vickie

One thing's for sure, we couldn't have done it without our friends all across the country. Each year, we're honored to turn thousands of your recipes into our collectible cookbooks. Our hope is that each book captures the stories and heart of all of you who have shared with us. Whether you've been with us since the beginning or are just discovering us, welcome to the **Gooseberry Patch** family!

Visit us online:

www.gooseberrypatch.com
1•800•854•6673

U.S. to Metric Recipe Equivalents

Volume Measurements

1/4 teaspoon	1 mL
1/2 teaspoon	2 mL
1 teaspoon	5 mL
1 tablespoon = 3 teaspoons	15 mL
2 tablespoons = 1 fluid ounce	30 mL
1/4 cup	60 mL
1/3 cup	75 mL
1/2 cup = 4 fluid ounces	125 mL
1 cup = 8 fluid ounces	250 mL
2 cups = 1 pint =16 fluid ounces	500 mL
4 cups − 1 quart	1 L

Weights

1 ounce	30 g
4 ounces	120 g
8 ounces	225 g
16 ounces = 1 pound	450 g

Oven Temperatures

300° F	150° C
325° F	160° C
350° F	180° C
375° F	190° C
400° F	200° C
450° F	230° C

Baking Pan Sizes

Square

8x8x2 inches	2 L = 20x20x5 cm
9x9x2 inches	2.5 L = 23x23x5 cm

Rectangular

13x9x2 inches	3.5 L = 33x23x5 cm

Loaf

9x5x3 inches	2 L = 23x13x7 cm

Round

8x1-1/2 inches	1.2 L = 20x4 cm
9x1-1/2 inches	1.5 L = 23x4 cm

Recipe Abbreviations

t. = teaspoon	ltr. = liter
T. = tablespoon	oz. = ounce
c. = cup	lb. = pound
pt. = pint	doz. = dozen
qt. = quart	pkg. = package
gal. = gallon	env. = envelope

Kitchen Measurements

A pinch = 1/8 tablespoon	1 fluid ounce = 2 tablespoons
3 teaspoons = 1 tablespoon	4 fluid ounces = 1/2 cup
2 tablespoons = 1/8 cup	8 fluid ounces = 1 cup
4 tablespoons = 1/4 cup	16 fluid ounces = 1 pint
8 tablespoons = 1/2 cup	32 fluid ounces = 1 quart
16 tablespoons = 1 cup	16 ounces net weight = 1 pound
2 cups = 1 pint	
4 cups = 1 quart	
4 quarts = 1 gallon	